anything

A+ books

Different Kinds of Good-byes

by Shelley Rotner and Sheila Kelly, EdD
photographs by Shelley Rotner

CAPSTONE PRESS
a capstone imprint

It's not always easy to say **good-bye.**

3

But there are many different kinds of **good-byes.**

There's "good-bye" to your **parents** when they take you to school.

There's "good-bye" to your **friends** when it's time to go home.

There's "good-bye" to **Gram** when you talk on the **phone**.

There's "good-bye"
to your **dog**
when you leave.

There's "good-bye" to your **driver** when she drops you at your stop.

There's "good-bye" to
the **clerk** at the store.

There's even "good-bye" to the **sun**.

It's hard to say **good-bye** when your parent goes out.

It's hard when your sister goes off to school.

15

It's hard to say **good-bye** when friends move **far away.**

VING SERVICES

17

When you live in
two homes,

there are **lots** of good-byes.

There's "good-bye" at the airport

and "good-bye" at the **train station.**

21

There's "good-bye" when you get on the bus.

The **hardest** good-bye is a good-bye that's forever.

But **pictures** help us remember the **happy times** together.

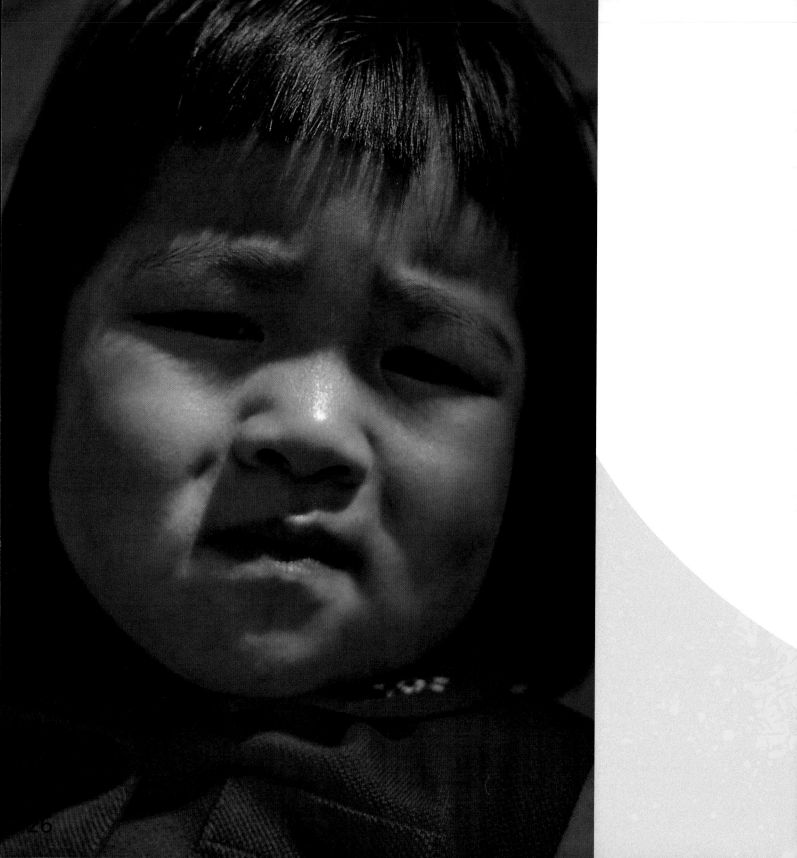

 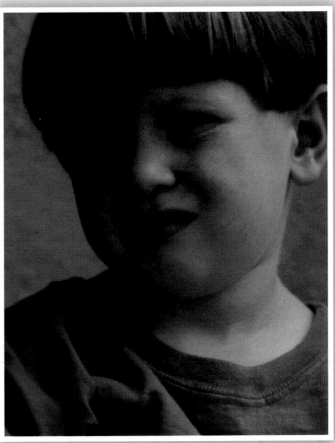

Good-byes can make you sad.

Good-byes can make you angry.

It can be **hard** to say **good-bye**...

but most good-byes are

"good-bye for now!"

A+ Books are published by Capstone Press,
1710 Roe Crest Drive, North Mankato, Minnesota 56003.
www.capstonepub.com

Library of Congress Cataloging-in-Publication Data
Rotner, Shelley.
 Different kinds of good-byes / by Shelley Rotner and Sheila Kelly.
    p. cm. — (A+ books. Shelley Rotner's world.)
 Summary: "Full-color photographs and simple text illustrate a variety of good-bye situations"—Provided
by publisher.
 ISBN 978-1-62065-066-0 (library binding)
 ISBN 978-1-62065-750-8 (paperback)
 ISBN 978-1-4765-1346-1 (ebook PDF)
1. Children—Juvenile literature. 2. Separation (Psychology) in children—Juvenile literature. 3. Farewells—Juvenile
literature. I. Kelly, Sheila M. II. Title.
 HQ781.R667 2013
 305.23—dc23   2012033986

Editorial Credits
Jill Kalz, editor; Heidi Thompson, designer; Wanda Winch, media researcher; Jennifer Walker, production specialist

Internet Sites

FactHound offers a safe, fun way to find Internet sites related to this book. All of the sites on FactHound have been researched by our staff.

Here's all you do:

Visit *www.facthound.com*

Type in this code: 9781620650660

Look for all the books in the series:

Different Kinds of Good-byes

Feeling Thankful

We All Do Something Well

What's Love?

Super-cool stuff! Check out projects, games and lots more at www.capstonekids.com

Printed in the United States of America in North Mankato, Minnesota.
092012   006933CGS13